I live in Stirling, Scotland, which is a truly beautiful part of the world surrounded by hills and countryside. I started writing poetry as a way to relax and record some of my life experiences, which lead to my first book being published in 2016. I was encouraged to write more children's poems, so I created *Puddlepond Lane*.

Puddlepond
Lane

Liz Gillespie

Puddlepond Lane

Nightingale Books

NIGHTINGALE PAPERBACK

© Copyright 2019
Liz Gillespie
Illustrations by Elena García Claro

A CIP catalogue record for this title is
available from the British Library.

ISBN 978 1 912021 48 2

*Nightingale Books is an imprint of
Pegasus Elliot MacKenzie Publishers Ltd.*
www.pegasuspublishers.com

First Published in 2019

**Nightingale Books
Sheraton House Castle Park
Cambridge England**

Printed & Bound in Great Britain

Dedication

This book is dedicated to all the children in the world. Even if you don't enjoy reading or have the opportunity to read as often as you would like, I hope you all follow your dreams and write your own exciting stories.

Acknowledgements

Thank you to my husband, Gavin, who supports and encourages me to follow all of my dreams. Thanks to my lovely group of proof readers and editors: Petrona, TJ, Fiona, Alan and of course, Gavin. And to the mums: Amanda, Leeann and Anne-Marie, who tested my stories with their own children.

Excuse me please, if you will
Do you have an hour to kill?
Is there a little time in your day?
Would you like to come this way?

I know a place you'd love to see
I promise that there is no fee
You will want to return time and again
Once you have visited Puddlepond Lane

A magical place, it's not very far
You don't even need to bring your car
Just sit down in your favourite nook
And start to read this enchanting book

You will meet new friends,have some fun
A happy place in rain or sun
Everyone is welcome here
A place I hold so very dear.

Up, Up and Away

Layla felt so very sad
It made her want to cry
Layla whispered to her dad
I fear I cannot fly

Now don't you fear oh chick of mine
Your feathers need to grow
You need more patience and in time
Your fluffy down will go

Your wings will grow much stronger
And your plumes will start to shine
Believe me chick when daddy says
You will fly, just give it time

Layla tried so very hard
She flapped her wings in vain
Each day she tried in her front yard
Then up and down the lane

She tried all kinds of different things
As her feathers slowly grew
She flapped her wings
Her hopes renewed

In the park a child ran by
His balloons escaped his grasp
They floated up into the sky
Layla jumped as they went past

She tried to grab them in her beak
As she flapped her wings so very fast
Then gathering up a little speed
Layla caught them with one last gasp

Oh my, she cried with great surprise
When she looked around
Layla's feet were tucked up tight
No longer on the ground

Layla rushed to tell her dad
He could see her teary eyes
But Layla was no longer sad
She said "I am a chicken and I can fly."

Tiny Little Snowdrop

Tiny little snowdrop
Surrounded with crisp white snow
Has woken way too early
Just keen to sprout and grow

Tiny little snowdrop
No need to bow your head
Your beauty is most welcome
In my little flower bed

A Blustery Day

One blustery day down
Puddlepond way
Henrietta opened her door

The leaves from the trees
flew about in the breeze
To make a pile upon her floor

She'd bundle up warm
against the late spring storm
To visit a friend down the lane

Up went her umbrella
to protect from the weather
And keep her head dry from the rain

I must try again
to visit Flo down the lane
When the weather is more pleasant you see

We like to catch up
with some cake and a cup
Of Flo's wonderful elderflower tea

Fey

Fey lives in the meadow,
close to Puddlepond Lane

She likes to play in the sunshine
and dance in the rain

She likes to fly on a breeze
with her pretty little wings

And lay in the grass
as the nightingale sings

Easter Fey

Easter time fills Fey with glee
As bunnies hide treats for all to see

She watches children as they have fun
Finding Easter eggs in the morning sun

Their baskets full with chocolate sweets
And other delightful little treats

Easter Bonnet

A bright sunny day
down Puddlepond Lane
Henrietta was all of a tizz

Her new Easter Bonnet
has a little bee on it
And she can hear it go bzz bzz bzz

Oh what shall we do,
the parade is about due
And I don't have a moment to spare

I don't want to harm you or even alarm you
But I haven't anything else I can wear

But after a while
the bee flew off with a smile
And thanked her for the use of her hat

I had to come see
said the little buzzy bee
Your bonnet's like a flowery mat

The Picnic

It was a warm summer day
down Puddlepond Lane
Henrietta was enjoying the sun

A friend passed her gate,
she shouted please wait
And was shown some baking they'd done

I am off to the park,
said Annie the Lark
To share this tasty seed bun

You can come too
I've invited a few
For a picnic, some games and some fun

Henrietta agreed,
that is just what I need
I can bring the cake I made just this morn

As she picked up her things
with a flap of her wings
She waddled across her neat lawn

They played in the sun
the whole village had come
This was a spectacular sight

Now it's time to go home
and the food is all gone
As dusk bid the day a goodnight

The friends parted with a hug
down to the last ladybug
They smiled as they went on their way

Everyone agreed with a shout,
there was no doubt
It was a wonderful picnic that day

Montgomery

Montgomery is a hielan' coo
Wi'a great big ginger coat
When the weather is aw' baltic
It keeps him braw and hoat

His horns they look like haundl' bars
From ma da's auld chopper bike
He's no like aw' the other coos
Ye'v no seen nothing like

Little Blackbird

I saw a little blackbird sitting
On a table by the tree
Looking so intently
I wondered what she could see

What has caught your eye today
On the ground beneath the tree
What has got your attention ma'am?
I had to see what you can see

The ground has started thawing, sir
Beneath the grand old tree
I am looking so intently
Can you see what I can see?

The earth it has awoken and
Life stirs beneath the tree
I am looking so intently, sir
For something nice to have for tea

Pretty Little Poppy

Pretty little red poppy
How beautiful you've grown
You overcame all the odds
And survived where you are sown

A splendid splash of colour
You brighten up the day
You're unaware of the joy you give
when people pass your way

Your strength is hidden deep within
Away from prying eyes
Your petals, bold and delicate
Despite your meagre size

Little Duckling

Little tiny duckling
Waddles down the lane
Off to meet her duckling friends
To play a little game

Little tiny duckling
Swimming in the pond
Together with her duckling friends
They sing a little song

Little tiny duckling
Quacking merrily
With all her little duckling friends
They are happy as can be

Little tiny ducklings
From the pond just down the lane
Will meet each other in the morn
For another little game

Black Velvet

Dark as the night
with velvety fur
Mischievous and fun,
there is no stopping her

She darts through the door,
to see who is home
Looking to play,
she won't leave you alone

Bouncing through the house
on her own little mission
Taking over your lap,
no need for permission

A playmate is required,
you have a look see
As she bounces on the head
of a sleepy Cookie

The toys lay around,
but no interest is paid
A live victim is required,
the challenge is made

A squat, a wiggle,
a pounce from the ground
Movement so swift
and not even a sound

A tumble of fur
all over the floor
A successful ambush
then exits the door

Fun is all over
as quick as a flash
Cookie now knows
it is safe to relax

April Showers Down
Puddlepond Lane

April showers
and springtime rain
A beautiful pond
down Puddlepond Lane

Lily pads big,
bright and green
Flowers are as pretty
as you've ever seen

A bullfrog sitting
out in the sun
Mayflies dancing
and having fun

A songbird sings
through the leaves of a tree
A peaceful sight
of tranquillity

I sit on a bench
that catches my eye
And watch white fluffy clouds
drift over the sky

A beautiful pond
down Puddlepond Lane
Comes alive after showers
and springtime rain

Come join me to watch
all the clouds drift by
I will be the one
with the smile and a sigh

Tasha

Tasha is a turtle dove
She visits us down Puddlepond Lane
She likes to sit high in the tree
But comes down when you call her name

Tasha likes to travel near and far
But visits every spring
I like to listen to her tales
From all her travelling

Can I Go Out to Play?

Can I go out to play Mummy?
The sun is shining bright
Can I go out to play today?
I'll be back before it's night

I want to go on a treasure hunt
With my friends from Puddlepond Lane
I want to be a pirate today
Jolly Jack will be my name

I want to run and jump around
And make Timmy walk the plank
I want to have fun with all my friends
Along the river bank

Can I go out to play today?
I have tidied up my toys
Can I go out to play Mummy?
I want to make lots of noise

I want to shout out really loud
The way the pirates do
I want to run and laugh today
You can even come too

Maisey

Maisey is a little field mouse
Who lives down Puddlepond Lane
By day she plays in fields of wheat
At night she dreams of yummy grain

Twitchy little whiskers
At the end of her twitchy nose
Nimbly climbing the stalks of grass
With her tiny little toes

She scurries along the hedgerows
Looking for tasty treats
Never bothering anyone
She is nervous of all she meets

Baby Belle

Little Belle so full of fun
Around the garden she likes to run

Her bright wee eyes so full of cheek
Looking for mischief and some hide and seek

She has a little inquisitive snout
It's forever in stuff when she is out

In garden pots all full of flowers
To warm wet dirt after summer showers

Dinner time and she's now been fed
Tired Baby Belle trots off to bed

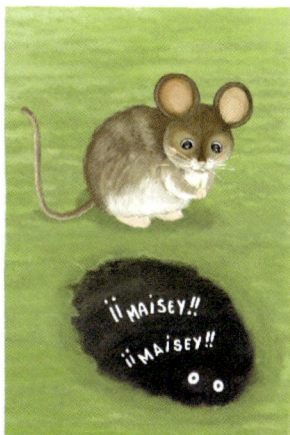

Maisey Saves the Day

One autumn day when she was out
In the hedgerows down the lane
She thought she heard a little squeak
And someone shout her name

Maisey stopped and looked around
But could not see a soul
Then she heard the sound again
From deep within a hole

Standing very still she heard
The voice it squeaked again
Help me Maisey I am trapped in here
Inside my little den

Maisey wanted to run and hide
Who was down that hole?
My oh my and deary me
Was it a field mouse eating troll?

Help me Maisey I can't get out
I have been trapped in here all day
If you help me get back out
You can scurry on your way

I cannot leave them there she thought
That's a frightened little voice
I have to help them get back out
I am afraid I have no choice

So nervously she dug right down
Until she could see its eyes
The voice is so much clearer now
I recognise those cries

Maisey had been very scared
And wanted to run away
Maisey had to be brave for once
And look – she saved the day

Who do you think was trapped in the hole?
Do you think anyone else would know?
Next time you visit Puddlepond Lane
Just ask who was trapped down below

Billie the Bullfrog

Billie is a bullfrog
with great big bulging eyes
He has a long and sticky tongue
that he uses to catch flies

Billie has a great big chin
he blows up like a balloon
And sings his happy bullfrog song
from morning until noon

I like to eat my flies ribbit ribbit
When I am sitting on the pond
I like to eat my flies ribbit ribbit
Singing my happy song

I like to eat my flies ribbit ribbit
I catch them with my tongue
I like to eat my flies ribbit ribbit
And now my song is sung

Billie is a bullfrog
he is happy on his pad
You will always hear his happy song
he is very seldom sad

Louie the Llama

Louie is a llama
Awaits beside the gate
If he thought you'd pat him on his head
He would gladly wait and wait

Louie used to live
In a land they call Peru
Now his home is Puddlepond Lane
He will tell you this is true

Louie is a llama
Still waiting by the gate
If you pass this way, please pat his head
He would gladly wait and wait

The Little Fox

I saw a little fox last night
he hurried past my sty
The red of his coat you see
was what had caught my eye

Whatever he was up to,
he gave me such a fright
I was woken up from my slumber
in the middle of the night

I have listened to the stories told
about this little guy
They make him out to be a thief,
he's sleekit and awfully sly

Do we really know him,
have you ever had a chat?
Don't listen to the tales
passed on by the cat

I bet he's just out when
no one else can see
He'll be looking for a snack
to take home for his tea

Rumours

I scurried past a pen last night
When no one was around
The noise that came from deep inside
Was a truly frightening sound

I've heard such stories from those I know
About a beast that lies within
A mean and dirty slavering thing
Who eats rubbish from a bin

I heard a grunt and snort and squeal
And did not want to wait
I thought it would eat me whole
From a dirty dinner plate

I had to slink by really fast
Almost crawling on the ground
I screwed my eyes until almost closed
And tried not to make a sound

I was only out this late at night
From my home beneath the tree
To stay away from the beasts around
While I fetch my cubs their tea

Parker the Pup

Parker was a barker
With a waggy little tail
He lived beside his master, Jack
On the farm down Puddlepond Lane

Parker was a barker
He liked to make a noise
He liked to play with his master, Jack
And all the pirate boys

Parker was a barker
He barked the whole day long
He barked and barked
Until something felt, well wrong!

Parker was a barker
But one day he lost his bark
He looked all over Puddlepond Lane
And a few times round the park

Parker, son, you barked too much
This just made him sad
Perhaps you've used it up, my son
Came the stern voice of his dad

You cannot go and bark all day
Without you paying a price
It hurts the ears of all your friends
It's really not that nice

Sometimes you need to be quiet, son
Pay attention to how others act
Barking for no reason will only hurt you
That my son, is a fact

Baby Owls

A little family of owls
Lives in Puddlepond tree
Will we count them
How many can you see?

Count them all
All you can see
Count them with me
1, 2, 3

Oculus, he is number 1
He likes to giggle just for fun
Opus must be number 2
He likes a hoot, twit woo

Oscar makes it number 3
He likes to sit high in the tree
Is that all that we can see?
Are there more in the tree?

Count them all
All you can see
Count them with me
1, 2, 3

Buzzy Honey Bee

I see a little honey bee
Upon a meadow flower
Gathering all the pollen
Avoiding an April shower

Such a busy little honey bee
Working all day long
Humming as you do your work
A buzzy little song

Bzz Bzz Bzz And Bzz Bzz Bzz
My work is never done
Bzz Bzz Bzz And Bzz Bzz Bzz
Working all day long

Now he flies off to his hive
With his collection for the day
To make some honey for his queen
In a buzzy kind of way

Such a busy little honey bee
Working all day long
Humming as he flies off home
A buzzy little song

Peek-a-Moo Coo

Peek-a-moo Boab
loves to play hide and seek
Once you hear him moo
you might see him peek

Peek-a-boo Boab
and his pal Wee Dunk
Sit and giggle all day long
behind a big tree trunk

Wee Dunk will give a giggle
and Boab a little moo
Then they peek from behind the trunk
looking straight at you

Do you want to play this game
with Boab and his pal Wee Dunk?
There is plenty space to
play behind the big tree trunk

Frosty Meadow

The meadow down by Puddlepond Lane
Is covered in a crisp white frost
And Fey is sitting in her home
Feeling a little lost

The frost is thick on the meadow grass
It's far too cold out there
The frost is covering everything
I have nothing warm to wear

My home is very cosy
With a fire burning in the hearth
To go outside I will need
A bobble hat and a scarf

Fey digs out some wool and pins
And sits down to her task
Before too long she's made a hat
Fey can knit things very fast

I want to make a pompom
To sit atop my hat
I will make it like a snowball
Big and white and fat

Then Fey starts to knit again
Her scarf begins to grow
A glance out of her window
Fey see it starts to snow

Before too long Fey has a scarf
To match her bobble hat
She adds a pompom to each end
Also, big and white and fat

Through the night as Fey slept
More snow fell all around
She smiled as she looked outside
The white blanket on the ground

In no time Fey is wrapped up warm
Wearing her new scarf and hat
She builds a great big snowman
Big and white and fat

All her friends join in to help
They had a lot of fun
A snowball fight to end the day
Can you guess who won?

Who's Hidden the Hyenas?

Who's hidden the hyenas?
I heard Wee Dunk shout

I have looked all over the place
And there is none of them about

I've looked in all the cages
In every corner of the zoo

I've looked all over the play park
And Alex has helped me too

I couldn't see them anywhere
But I can hear them laugh at me

I looked in all the cages
And even up a tree

So, who's hidden the hyenas?
I want to see them laugh

But now I don't have time to look
Mum says I need my bath

Springtime in Puddlepond Lane

Springtime in the farmer's fields
And look what we can see
Lots of little fluffy lambs
Leaping and jumping about with glee

Little fluffy tails ablur
All wiggling with delight
Lambs all playing in the field
What a lovely sight

The Beautiful Blue String

One day when I was walking
I found a piece of string
I stared at it for quite some time
It was such a lovely thing

It was made from long and silky thread
With a knot or two
Its colour reminded me of the sky
Such a lovely shade of blue

I wondered where it came from
And how it came to be
Lying on the pavement
Just in front of me

I imagined all the lovely things
It could have been a part of
Perhaps a magical floating carpet
Flying high above

Do you think it held the braids
In a unicorn's rainbow mane?
Or fell from the shawl of the fairy queen
who lives down Puddlepond Lane?

Some say it is a thread
That ties together dreams
Or kept the clouds up in the sky
Away from sunny beams

So many things it could have been
Too many for us to note
I think I will keep it to discuss again
Inside the pocket of my coat

The Fairy Queen's Shawl

A beautiful view,
as the day breaks anew
And dew settles fresh the meadow

The flowers awaken,
the low branches all taken
And birdsong is heard from the hedgerow

From far and from near,
we listen and hear
The plans they all have for their day

The far end of the lane,
there's puddles from rain
The Queen is out looking for Fey

She has a small task,
a favour to ask
To look in Fey's bag full of treasure

A piece of thread's what I need,
may I please take a peek?
My Queen it would be an immense pleasure

I have a small tear,
my shawl needs a repair
Just here on the edge, as you can see

There is no one I know
who would be better to sew
Could you help and sew this for me?

After looking around,
nothing was found
Not one of the threads here was blue

Fey scratched her head,
and looked under her bed
Then suddenly she knew what to do

My friend Honor will know
just where to go
To find some silken blue thread

Indeed, she knew just the place
and with a smile on her face
Said Sally Spider's spectacular web

She'll spin a thread just for you,
the perfect shade, the perfect hue
Her shop is just there down the lane

So off Fey ran,
as fast as she can
running through puddles in the rain

Sally made a thread,
of blue from her web
Without any trouble at all

Fey could now sew
with the thread of silken blue
The small tear in the Fairy Queen's shawl

Riddlepond Farm

Introduction to the Places and Characters

The Places

Puddlepond Lane

Puddlepond Lane is a picture postcard community filled with lots of lovely characters and places to visit. It has a farm, a lovely big park with a meadow and a big hill with an old oak tree on it. There is a large pond at the far end of the meadow and it all reminds you of chocolate box cottages and rose gardens where everyone helps everyone else.

Farm house

The farm house is a big old building with stables, barns, sheds and surrounded by lots of big open fields. There is a paddock at the side of the building just on the lane and this is where Louie lives. On the other side is the sty where Higgy and Belle live. The farmer, his wife, and their little boy Jack, all live in the farm house with their sheepdogs and cat.

The Meadow

In the summer the meadow is always full of beautiful wild flowers and in the winter it is a great place to build snowmen and have snowball fights. Fey lives in the meadow and looks after everything that grows there all year round.

The Tree

On top of the hill in the park is very large old oak tree. The tree is the home to lots of different characters and is a central place for everyone to meet up especially for picnics. Orlagh and her boys live high up in the branches while the little fox and her cubs live in a den deep below the roots.

The Pond

This is where Billie lives. It is a beautiful pond with lily pads in the centre and bulrushes around the edge. Jack likes to visit the pond with his mum to feed the ducks. He always takes a big bag of bread, the kind with lots of seeds in that that his mother makes every Sunday.

The Characters

Annie

Annie is a lark and friends with Henrietta. Annie lives in the big tree in the park and likes to organise picnics when the sun is shining. There are always games to be played, food to be eaten and lots of chatting and twittering.

Belle

Belle is an inquisitive little pig who likes to stick her nose into anything and everything. Belle lives at the sty beside Higgy.

Billie

Billie is a big happy bullfrog and lives on the pond. Billie loves to sit on his lily pad singing songs, eating flies and watching the world go by.

Boab

Boab is a young heifer who lives in a field with a big old highland coo called Monty. Boab has a wee friend called Dunk who likes to play hide and seek whenever he visits Boab.

Fey

Fey is a pretty, little fairy who looks after the flowers, plants, shrubs and trees in Puddlepond Lane but likes to daydream more than work. She is a favourite of the Fairy Queen so is often called upon to do some special tasks.

Henrietta

Henrietta is an elegant duck who seems to get into a never-ending string of adventures and mishaps. Henrietta lives near the pond with her brothers, sisters, nephews and nieces.

Honey Bee

Honey is a honey bee and lives in an apiary kept by the farmer's wife. Honey loves to visit pretty flowers to collect their pollen to make honey. Sometimes Honey will get distracted if she sees a pretty place to rest and has been seen to rest on Henrietta's Easter Bonnet as it is so pretty.

Jack

Jack is the little boy who lives in the farm house. He loves playing outside and going on adventures with his friends.

Layla

Layla is a chicken who thought she could not fly but always dreamed of being able to soar above the tree tops. With a lot of perseverance, advice and help from her friends and family she discovered not just how to fly but so much more. Layla lives at the coop at the back of the farm house.

Little Fox

Little Fox lives under the big tree with his cubs. He fears the hidden beast who lives in the sty next to the farm house.

Louie the Llama

Louie is a llama who was born in a country far away called Peru. He lives in a small field next to the farm. He likes to wait at the gate for pats from passers-by.

Maisey

Maisey is a courageous little field mouse who is nervous of everything. Maisey lives in a cosy little mouse hole close to the fields.

Montgomery the Highland Coo

Monty to his friends. Monty lives in the field at the end of the lane opposite the pond. He shares his field with a young heifer called Boab who likes to play hide and seek with his friend Dunk.

Oculus, Opus and Oscar

Three little owl brothers who live in the tree in the park next to the pond.

Orlagh

Orlagh is a very large tawny owl. She has lived in the tree in the park for many years and knows everyone who lives in Puddlepond Lane. Orlagh has three young sons called Oculus, Opus and Oscar.

Parker

Parker is a very loud and bouncy sheepdog pup with a very waggy tail. Parker and his mum and dad all live with Jack and his family in the farm house.

Higgy the Hog

Higgy the Hog is a very large pig who lives at the sty next to the farm house. He likes to stay in his hut at night where it is warm and cozy. Higgy is known to snore, snort and grunt when he is sleeping, making him sound like a monster, and he wishes he could stop because he is not a monster really. Higgy shares his sty with a young pig called Bella.

Sally Spider

Sally is a fine spinner of silks and has a shop just down the lane. The Fairy Queen often asks Sally to spin her the thread for her royal shawls as the colours are so bright and beautiful.

Velvet

Velvet is the farm cat. Her fur is black as midnight and velvet smooth. She loves to wiggle and pounce all over the place but returns to a warm hearth at the farm house every night. She has a friend called Cookie who is a house cat and does not like to go out very much.

Little Duckling

Little Duckling is a nephew of Henrietta and lives close to the pond. He likes to waddle up the lane to visit his friends and loves to paddle in the pond.

Little Blackbird

Little Blackbird lives in the big tree. You might see her digging about in the soft ground looking for yummy treats for her tea.

Tasha

Tasha is a turtle dove who likes to travel all over the world. She visits Puddlepond Lane to catch up with her friends and to tell them stories about the countries she has visited.

The Hyenas

No one knows where the hyenas live as nobody has ever found them. If you listen very carefully you might hear them laugh and laugh but you might never see them.